ISBN-13: 9798853275331
ISBN-10: 1477123456

Cover design by: Art Painter
Library of Congress Control Number: 2018675309
Printed in the United States of America

CONTENTS

SMART MONEY KIDS: TEACHING FINANCIAL FREEDOM EARLY

By Jacquez Brown

AUTHOR'S NOTE:

Dear readers,

Thank you for joining Tim and Emma on their magical money adventure! It has been an absolute joy to share their journey with you.

As an author, my goal was to create a fun and creative story that not only entertained but also sparked curiosity and inspired a love for learning about money.

Money is often seen as a serious and grown-up topic, but Tim and Emma's story shows that it can be exciting, adventurous, and filled with magic. By exploring the world of finance through their eyes, we can discover the true value of money—how it can help us achieve our dreams, make a positive impact, and build a better future.

I hope that this story has ignited a spark in your hearts and minds, encouraging you to embark on your own money adventure. Remember, whether you're saving for a goal, investing in your future, or giving back to others, every step you take is a valuable part of your journey.

So, keep asking questions, keep seeking knowledge, and never stop exploring the wonders of the financial world. Your adventure is waiting, and the possibilities are endless!

Until we meet again on the next thrilling

page, Happy reading and happy money

adventuring! With warm regards, Jacquez

Brown

BOOK INTRODUCTION:

Hey there, parents and guardians!

Are you tired of hearing "Can I have that?" or "I want this!" every time you take your kids to the store? Do you wish your little ones understood the value of money and how to manage it responsibly? Well, you're in for a treat! "Smart Money Kids: Teaching Financial Freedom Early" is here to help you raise money-savvy children who can handle their finances with confidence and even enjoy the process!

In today's fast-paced world, financial literacy is an essential skill. However, most schools don't teach it early on, leaving children to navigate the complex world of money without proper guidance. But fear is not! This book is packed with creative and interactive ways to introduce financial concepts to your kids in a fun, engaging manner.

As we embark on this adventure together, we'll explore fifteen exciting chapters that are designed to unleash the inner financial genius in your children. From the wonders of piggy banks to the thrilling journey of investing in the candy stock market, we'll cover it all!

We believe that financial education shouldn't be boring or complicated, and that's why we've adopted an informal and creative writing style. Our goal is to empower you to spark meaningful conversations with your kids about money, and together, build a solid foundation for their financial future.

So, let's dive right in and explore how to instruct your kids about financial freedom early, turning them into the smart money kids of tomorrow!

CHAPTER 1: PIGGY BANK ADVENTURES

Once upon a time, in a land not so far away, there lived a little boy named Tim and a little girl named Emma. Tim and Emma were eager to learn about money and how to take care of it. That's when they discovered the magical world of piggy banks!

Their journey began when their parents gifted them each a cute, colorful piggy bank. Tim's piggy bank was blue with a big grin, and Emma's was pink with rosy cheeks. The siblings were excited to start saving their money, but they didn't know where to begin.

Fortunately, their wise grandma, Nana May, came to the rescue. Nana May was a financial expert, and she knew just how to teach Tim and Emma about the magic of saving. She sat them down and said, "Listen closely, my dear ones. Your piggy banks are more than just cute toys. They are the secret to unlocking the power of money!"

Tim and Emma's eyes widened with curiosity. Nana May continued, "Every time you receive money—whether it's from your allowance, gifts, or doing chores—you can place a portion of it into your piggy banks. It may seem like a small amount at first, but over time, it will grow and grow, just like a magic beanstalk!"The kids were thrilled by the idea of raising their money like magic. From that day on, Tim and Emma diligently put their spare change into their piggy banks. They even started doing extra chores to earn more money to save.

As the months went by, Tim and Emma's piggy banks grew heavier, and they couldn't wait to see how much money they had saved. Nana May taught them the joy of delayed gratification, explaining that by waiting patiently, their money would grow even more. It was a valuable lesson that they carried with them throughout their lives.

One day, after saving for many months, Tim and Emma decided it was time to open their piggy banks and count their treasure. They sat on the living room floor, surrounded by stacks of shiny coins. Excitement filled the air as they popped open their piggy banks and poured out the contents.

To their amazement, they had saved enough money to buy a special gift for their parents—a heartfelt thank-you for all the love and care they received. Tim and Emma realized that saving money not only made them feel proud, but it also gave them the power to make dreams come true.

And so, the adventure of Tim and Emma's piggy bank continued, teaching them valuable lessons about money, patience, and the joy of saving. Little did they know that their journey was just beginning, and there were many more magical financial adventures waiting for them in the pages ahead.

CHAPTER 2: THE GREAT PENNY CHALLENGE

After their fantastic piggy bank adventure, Tim and Emma couldn't wait to embark on their next financial escapade. Nana May had something exciting in store for them—the Great Penny Challenge!

Nana May handed each of them a small glass jar and said with a mischievous twinkle in her eye, "Alright, kiddos, it's time for the penny challenge! Your mission, should you choose to accept it, is to collect as many pennies as you can find. The catch? You can only use pennies, no other coins!"

Tim and Emma giggled with excitement. "That sounds like so much fun, Nana!" Emma exclaimed, clutching her jar tightly. "But what's the goal of this challenge?" Tim asked, intrigued.

Nana May smiled and replied, "The goal is to see who can fill their jar with the most pennies. But there's a twist! The pennies you collect will go to a good cause of your choice."

The siblings loved the idea of helping others while having a blast. They at once started hunting for pennies everywhere they went—on sidewalks, in parking lots, and even beneath sofa cushions. Tim once found a penny in the garden, buried like treasure, and Emma discovered a lucky penny on her way to school.

As the weeks went by, their penny jars began to fill up. They even got creative, making a game out of spotting pennies during family outings. "Look, Emma! There's a penny by the ice cream truck!" Tim would shout, and they'd both scramble to grab it.

Nana May was delighted by their enthusiasm. "You two are doing great!" she praised. "Remember, it's not just about the number of pennies. It's about the joy of giving back and making a difference."

When the challenge ended, Tim and Emma gathered around the kitchen table, jars in hand, to count their pennies. The suspense was electrifying as they poured out their collections. Emma's jar cost 378 pennies, and Tim's had 415!
"Wow, Tim, you won!" Emma exclaimed, clapping her hands. Tim blushed and grinned proudly, but then he had an idea. "You know what, Emma? Let's combine our pennies and donate them together."

Emma's eyes lit up. "That's a fantastic idea, Tim!" So, they added their pennies together and decided to give the money to a local animal shelter. Nana May beamed with pride, seeing how much they had learned about generosity and teamwork.

They proudly handed the donation to the shelter, where they got to meet some furry friends who received help from their penny challenge. The experience filled their hearts with warmth, knowing that their efforts had helped the animals.

The Great Penny Challenge taught Tim and Emma that even small contributions could make a significant difference in the lives of others. They realized that being financially smart was not just about saving for themselves but also about using money to do good in the world.

As they continued their financial journey, Tim and Emma discovered that there were countless creative ways to learn about money while having fun. With every adventure, they became more confident in their ability to manage money wisely and make a positive impact.

And so, their smart money kids' journey continued, brimming with laughter, lessons, and the joy of learning together. Stay tuned for more exciting chapters as Tim and Emma explore the world of financial literacy and discover the true meaning of financial freedom!

CHAPTER 3: MONEY TALK AT THE DINNER TABLE

"**D**inner's ready!" Mom called out from the kitchen, and the family gathered around the table, eager to dig into a delicious meal. But tonight, something was different. Tonight, there was going to be a "money talk" at the dinner table!

Tim and Emma exchanged curious glances. "What's the money talk, Mom?" Tim asked, his fork poised in mid-air. "Well, kiddos," Mom began, "it's time for us to have a little chat about money—how we earn it, how we spend it, and how we save it."

Dad chimed in, "That's right! Money is an important part of our lives, and it's essential for us to understand how it works." Tim and Emma nodded, suddenly feeling like they were in on some grown-up secret.

Mom started the conversation by explaining that money didn't grow on trees, and it took challenging work to earn it. "Dad and I work to earn money, and that's how we can afford to buy groceries, pay bills, and take care of our family," she said.

Emma's eyes widened, and she asked, "Can we earn money too?" Mom smiled and replied, "Absolutely! You can start by doing some extra chores around the house, like helping with the dishes or cleaning your room. We can give you a small allowance for your efforts."

Tim's mind was buzzing with ideas. "And what about saving money?" he asked. Dad leaned in and said, "Saving money is like planting seeds for the future.

When you set aside some of your earnings instead of spending it all, you'll have a nice little nest egg that can grow over time."

Emma piped up, "But it's so tempting to spend money on toys and treats!" Mom nodded knowingly. "It's completely natural to want things, Emma," she said. "That's where learning about needs versus wants comes in. We have to prioritize our spending on things we truly need, like food and clothing, before spending on things we want."
Dad added with a grin, "But don't worry, you can still treat yourself to something fun once in a while. It's all about finding a balance." Tim and Emma felt reassured, knowing that they could enjoy some treats without feeling guilty.

As the family chatted away, the dinner table turned into a money school of sorts. They learned about budgeting, setting financial goals, and the importance of giving back to the community through donations or volunteering.

Mom shared a story about her childhood when she saved up for weeks to buy a special toy she really wanted. "It felt so rewarding to buy it with my hard-earned money," she reminisced. "That's a great feeling, and I want you both to experience it too."

With their minds buzzing with newfound knowledge, Tim and Emma realized that money wasn't something to be afraid of—it was a tool they could use wisely to achieve their dreams and make a difference in the world.

From that day on, money talk became a regular feature at the dinner table. Each member of the family shared their financial triumphs, challenges, and what they had learned. They celebrated every milestone, whether it was reaching a savings goal or finding a clever way to stretch their money further.

As Tim and Emma grew older, they continued to develop their money skills, making smart financial decisions and working towards their dreams. And even when they faced tough times, they knew they could rely on their family's support and their own financial ability to overcome any obstacle.

So, the dinner table became not just a place to enjoy tasty meals but also a space to share, learn, and grow as smart money kids. And as their journey continued, Tim and Emma discovered that the most valuable currency in the world wasn't just dollars and cents—it was the knowledge and confidence to navigate the world of money with wisdom and joy.

CHAPTER 4: THE ABCS OF SAVING

One sunny Saturday morning, Tim and Emma woke up feeling extra curious. They had heard about the ABCs of saving from their teacher at school, and they couldn't wait to find out what it meant. So, they dashed downstairs to the living room, where Nana May was sipping her morning coffee.

"Nana, Nana, guess what we learned at school? The ABCs of saving!" Emma exclaimed, her eyes shining with excitement. Nana May chuckled warmly, setting down her cup. "Ah, the ABCs of saving, huh? Well, I'm glad you're eager to learn. Sit down, and I'll tell you all about it."

Tim and Emma plopped down on the couch, ready for Nana's wisdom. "The ABCs of saving are like a secret code to help you become super-savers!" Nana began, a playful glint in her eye. "Each letter stands for a different rule that will help you save money like pros."

"Awesome! Let's hear them!" Tim said, leaning forward with enthusiasm. Nana May nodded and started with 'A': "A stands for 'Always Pay Yourself First.' Whenever you receive money, whether it's from your allowance or doing extra chores, make sure to set aside a part for savings right away. It's like giving a little gift to your future self!"

Emma chimed in, "B must be for 'Budgeting,' right?" Nana May smiled and nodded, "You got it, Emma! B stands for 'Budget Your Money Wisely.' Keep track of your spending and decide how much to distribute for different things. This way, you won't spend all your money in one go."

"Now comes 'C,' which stands for 'Cut Unnecessary Expenses,'" Nana continued. "Sometimes we buy things we don't really need. By cutting back on those extra expenses, you'll have more money to save and invest in things that truly matter to you."

Tim scratched his head, pondering the next letter. "I think I know the 'D' already! It's 'Debt is a No-No,' right?" Nana May chuckled, "You're absolutely right, Tim! D stands for 'Avoid Debt.' Try not to borrow money or get into debt that you can't easily pay back. It's better to save up for what you want."

With excitement, Emma shouted, "E must stand for 'Emergency Fund!'" Nana May nodded proudly, "You're on fire today, Emma! He stands for 'Establish an Emergency Fund.' Life is full of surprises, and it's wise to have some money set aside for unexpected situations. It'll give you peace of mind."

"Now, the last letter is 'F,'" Tim said, eagerly waiting to hear the final rule. Nana May smiled warmly, "You're right, Tim! F stands for 'Focus on Your Goals.' When you have a savings goal in mind, like buying a new bike or saving for college, it becomes easier to resist unnecessary spending."

As Tim and Emma absorbed the wisdom of the ABCs of saving, they felt like they were uncovering the secrets to a treasure map. They couldn't wait to put these rules into action and become super-savers.

With Nana May as their guide, they started saving even more diligently, creating their very own piggy bank challenge to see who could save the most in a month. They set up a budget for their allowance, cutting back on little treats to save for something bigger.

And when unexpected situations arose, like a broken toy or a surprise school trip, they dipped into their emergency fund instead of worrying their parents.

As the weeks went by, Tim and Emma watched their savings grow steadily. They knew that with the ABCs of saving as their secret code, they were well on their way to mastering the art of money management.

And so, with newfound knowledge and determination, Tim and Emma continued their journey towards financial freedom. With each step they took, they knew that the ABCs of saving were their guiding stars, leading them towards a bright and secure future.

CHAPTER 5: FUN MONEY AND RESPONSIBILITY

Tim and Emma were over the moon with their growing savings, but they also knew that money wasn't just about saving—it was also about having some fun! Nana May believed that it was essential to strike a balance between saving and spending, so she decided to introduce them to the concept of "Fun Money."

"What's fun money, Nana?" Emma asked, her eyes sparkling with curiosity. Nana May grinned, "Fun money is a special portion of your allowance or earnings that you can use to treat yourself to little pleasures. It's like giving yourself permission to have a bit of fun with your money!"

The idea of fun money intuitively appealed to Tim and Emma. They envisioned all the things they could buy—a shiny new toy, a delicious ice cream cone, or maybe even a cool gadget. But Nana May had a surprise for them.

"Now, here's the twist," Nana said, raising an eyebrow playfully. "Fun money comes with a bit of responsibility. You get to decide how to spend it, but you also must think carefully about your choices. Remember, it's not an endless supply of money, so choose wisely!"

Tim and Emma nodded, realizing that even fun money required thoughtful decision-making. They decided to create a "Fun Money Wishlist." On this list, they wrote down all the things they wanted to buy with their fun money.

"I want a remote-controlled race car!" Tim exclaimed, scribbling it down on his list. Emma smiled and said, "I'd love a beautiful new sketchbook and some colorful art supplies!"

The siblings were thrilled with their fun money Wishlist's and started saving up for their desired treats. Every time they received their allowances, they would set aside a part for fun money and watch their little stash grow.

As the weeks passed, they faced some tough choices. Should Tim buy the race car he had been eyeing for months, or should he save a little more to get an even better one? Emma had to decide whether to buy the sketchbook now or wait for a sale to get the art supplies too.

In the end, they both realized that delaying gratification was worth it. Tim saved a bit more and was thrilled to buy the race car of his dreams, and Emma waited for a sale and got a fabulous deal on her sketchbook and art supplies.

Nana May was impressed with their thoughtful approach to spending their fun money. "You both are becoming real money experts!" she praised. "Remember, it's not just about how much money you have—it's about making smart choices and finding joy in both saving and spending."

With each experience, Tim and Emma felt more confident in their financial decision-making skills. They learned that fun money wasn't just about buying things—it was about the joy of making choices and being responsible with their money.

As they continued their money adventure, they discovered that there were many creative ways to have fun without spending a lot. They organized family game nights, made homemade gifts for each other, and had picnics in the park.

They even started an "Acts of Kindness" jar, where they would use some of their fun money to do small acts of kindness for others, like buying a friend a surprise treat or donating to a charity they cared about.

Through the journey of fun, money and responsibility, Tim and Emma learned that money was a powerful tool that could bring joy not just to themselves but also to those around them. They felt a newfound sense of empowerment, knowing that they could make a positive impact with their money choices.

And so, with their fun money Wishlist's in hand and hearts filled with excitement, Tim and Emma continued their money adventure, ready to embrace the joy of saving, the thrill of spending, and the magic of responsible money management.

CHAPTER 6: ENTREPRENEURIAL LEMONADE STAND

On a scorching summer day, Tim and Emma were feeling the heat, but they also had a brilliant idea to beat it—an entrepreneurial lemonade stand!

"What do you think, Emma? A lemonade stand would be the perfect way to make some money and cool off at the same time!" Tim said, his eyes gleaming with excitement. Emma nodded eagerly, "You're right, Tim! And we can use the money we make to add to our fun money stash!"

Nana May was thrilled with their entrepreneurial spirit. "That's a fantastic idea, kids! Let's get this lemonade stand up and running!" she said, rolling up her sleeves.

The trio worked together to set up the stand in their front yard, complete with a colorful banner that read "Tim and Emma's Cool Lemonade Stand!" They stocked up on lemons, sugar, and ice, and Nana May showed them how to make the perfect pitcher of lemonade.

As the first customers approached, Tim and Emma felt a mix of nervousness and excitement. "Lemonade, ice-cold lemonade! Get your refreshing lemonade here!" they called out, waving to passersby.

Their friendly smiles and enthusiasm were infectious, and soon enough, customers began flocking to their stand. Some were neighbors who stopped by out of curiosity, while others were kids who wanted a refreshing treat on a sweltering day.

Tim and Emma quickly got the hang of being young entrepreneurs. They poured lemonade with care, chatted with customers about their day, and even threw in a free cookie with every purchase. "A happy customer is a repeat customer!" Nana May whispered, and the siblings nodded in agreement.

Business was booming, and word of their delicious lemonade spread like wildfire. Soon, they had a line of eager customers, patiently waiting for their turn to enjoy the cool, tangy drink.
As the day went on, Tim and Emma saw their hard work pay off. Their tip jar overflowed with coins, and they couldn't help but feel a sense of pride in what they had achieved.

But the lemonade stand wasn't just about making money—it was also about learning valuable lessons. Nana May took the opportunity to teach them about pricing, expenses, and even a bit of marketing.

She encouraged them to track their sales and calculate their earnings, helping them understand the concept of profit and loss. "You two are little business moguls in the making!" Nana May said, beaming with pride.

At the end of the day, after the last drop of lemonade was poured, Tim and Emma sat down with Nana May to count their earnings. They couldn't believe their eyes—what started as a simple lemonade stand had turned into a successful business venture!

But the best part was yet to come. As they sat together, sipping their own lemonade, they realized that the money they had made meant more than just extra cash—it was a symbol of their hard work, creativity, and teamwork.

With a twinkle in her eye, Nana May said, "You see, kids, being an entrepreneur isn't just about making money. It's about using your imagination, taking risks, and putting in the effort to turn an idea into reality."

Tim and Emma nodded, realizing that their lemonade stand adventure had taught them valuable life skills. They learned that with a little courage and determination, they could turn their passions into something amazing.

As the sun set on their lemonade stand, Tim and Emma felt a sense of accomplishment that warmed their hearts as much as their lemonade cooled their bodies. They knew that this was just the beginning of their entrepreneurial journey, and they were excited to see where it would take them next.

And so, with the taste of success and a newfound entrepreneurial spirit, Tim and Emma continued their money adventure, ready to take on new challenges, embrace new opportunities, and turn every idea into a lemonade stand of possibilities.

CHAPTER 7: THE POWER OF DELAYED GRATIFICATION

One rainy afternoon, Tim and Emma found themselves cozied up indoors with a dilemma. They had been saving up for a special video game console, but they were tempted to spend their money on a cool new toy that just hit the stores.

"Emma, this new toy looks amazing! I really want it," Tim said, eyeing the shiny packaging with longing. Emma agreed, "I know, Tim, but we've been saving up for the game console for a while now. It's hard to decide!"

Nana May, always ready with wise advice, joined the conversation. "Ah, the power of delayed gratification!" she exclaimed. "It's the ability to resist the temptation of immediate rewards and instead wait for something even better."

Tim and Emma listened intently as Nana May shared a story from her childhood. "When I was about your age," she began, "I saved up for weeks to buy a beautiful, handcrafted wooden dollhouse. But one day, I saw a flashy new toy in the store, and I was tempted to buy it instead."

She continued, "But my mom reminded me about the power of delayed gratification. She said that if I waited a little longer and stuck to my original goal of buying the dollhouse, I would have something truly special and meaningful."

Tim and Emma's eyes widened, realizing the value of waiting for something they genuinely wanted. "So, you're saying we should wait for the video game console, Nana?" Emma asked.

Nana May smiled warmly, "It's ultimately your decision, my dear. But I want you to consider the joy of achieving a long-term goal. Waiting a little longer may bring you even more satisfaction and happiness."

Tim and Emma thought about it, and something inside them clicked. They decided to hold off on buying the new toy and stick to their original plan of saving for the video game console.

With renewed determination, they set up a "Delayed Gratification Chart" on the wall. Every day they resisted the temptation to buy the new toy, they marked off a day on the chart. Each day they moved closer to their goal, they felt a sense of accomplishment that outweighed the allure of the new toy.

As the days turned into weeks, their savings grew steadily, and they got even more excited about the console they were about to own. They imagined the endless hours of fun they would have playing their favorite games together.

Finally, the day came when they had saved enough money to buy the video game console. Tim and Emma marched into the store, money in hand, and bought their long-awaited treasure.

As they set up the console at home and started playing their favorite games, they knew they had made the right decision. The joy they felt was more than just the excitement of a new toy—it was the satisfaction of achieving a goal they had worked hard for.

Nana May was overjoyed to see how much they had learned about delayed gratification. "You see, kids, patience and perseverance can lead to even greater rewards than instant satisfaction," she said.

Tim and Emma couldn't agree more. They realized that delayed gratification wasn't just about waiting—it was about the journey of discipline, determination, and the sweet victory of achieving their dreams.

And so, armed with the power of delayed gratification, Tim and Emma continued their money adventure with a newfound appreciation for long-term goals and the joy of savoring every step of the way.

CHAPTER 8: INVESTING FOR KIDS: THE CANDY STOCK MARKET

Tim and Emma were always on the lookout for exciting ways to learn about money, and one day, they stumbled upon a unique opportunity—the Candy Stock Market!

"What's the Candy Stock Market, Nana?" Tim asked, intrigued by the idea of investing in candy. Nana May explained with a twinkle in her eye, "Well, it's a fun and educational game where you get to buy and sell candy 'stocks' as if they were real shares in a company!"

Emma giggled, "So, we get to be candy tycoons? That sounds awesome!" Nana May nodded, "Exactly! You'll each get a certain amount of 'money' to invest, and then you can buy several types of candy at varying prices. As the prices change, you can sell them and make a profit!"

Tim and Emma were thrilled to try it. They set up their candy stock market at the kitchen table, with a bowl of colorful candies standing for different stocks. Nana May acted as the candy market broker, updating the prices based on the candies' demand.

With their "investment funds" in hand, they began making strategic candy purchases. Tim went for gummy bears, while Emma invested in lollipops. Each day, they eagerly checked the stock market prices, making decisions based on the fluctuations.

As they played the game, they learned about the concepts of supply and demand, as well as the importance of staying informed about market trends. They also discovered that sometimes it was better to hold onto their candies and wait for the right moment to sell, just like real investors.

But the most valuable lesson they learned was the element of risk. "Sometimes the prices go up, and sometimes they go down," Emma said, frowning as she saw the value of her lollipops drop. "That's true, Emma," Nana May said gently. "Investing involves some risk, and it's essential to be prepared for both gains and losses."

As the weeks went by, Tim and Emma's candy portfolios fluctuated wildly. Sometimes they celebrated big profits, and other times they learned from their losses. But through it all, they had a blast and gained a deeper understanding of the world of finance.

They even decided to create their very own "candy company," coming up with a clever name and designing their candy packaging. They learned about marketing and branding, and soon, their candy stocks became the most sought- after in the market.

Nana May was delighted to see their enthusiasm for investing and finance. "You two are natural entrepreneurs and investors!" she exclaimed. "Remember, the world of finance is full of opportunities and exciting challenges. With each experience, you'll grow wiser and more confident."

Tim and Emma felt like they had unlocked a whole new world of possibilities. The Candy Stock Market had taught them valuable skills they could use in real-life situations. They now understood the importance of patience, research, and making informed decisions when it came to money matters.

As they wrapped up their Candy Stock Market game, Tim and Emma knew that their money adventure was far from over. They had tasted the thrill of investing and discovered a passion for understanding how money worked.

With their hearts brimming with excitement, they looked forward to exploring even more financial adventures, ready to embrace the twists and turns that would come their way.

And so, armed with the lessons of the Candy Stock Market and a growing appetite for financial knowledge, Tim and Emma continued their money journey, eager to uncover the secrets of the financial world one sweet step at a time.

CHAPTER 9: CHORES FOR DOUGH: EARNING AND BUDGETING

As Tim and Emma's financial knowledge expanded, they became curious about ways to earn more money and take charge of their finances. That's when Nana May introduced them to the concept of "Chores for Dough."

"Chores for Dough? Tell us more, Nana!" Emma said she was eager to learn how she could make some extra cash. Nana May explained, "Chores for Dough is a fun way to earn money by doing household tasks and taking on responsibilities."

Tim's eyes lit up, "So, if we help out more around the house, we can earn money?" Nana May nodded, "Exactly! It's a win-win situation. You get to earn some dough, and Mom and Dad get some help with chores. It teaches you the value of hard work and responsibility."

With Nana May's guidance, they created a chore chart with different tasks and their corresponding "earnings." Simple tasks like setting the table earned a few coins, while more significant tasks like mowing the lawn had a bigger reward.

Tim and Emma eagerly took on their new roles as chore enthusiasts. They swept the floors, watered the plants, and even took turns doing the dishes. With each completed chore, they felt a sense of pride in their efforts.

As the days went by, they accumulated a small pile of earnings. They decided to divide their money into three parts: saving, spending, and giving. "Saving is like planting seeds for the future," Tim said, placing a part of his earnings in his piggy bank.

Emma nodded, "And spending is like enjoying the fruits of our labor!" She excitedly thought about what she could buy with her money. Nana May smiled, "That's right! But don't forget about giving back too."

Nana May suggested they choose a cause they cared about and set aside some money for donations or charity. "It's a wonderful way to make a positive impact on others," she said.

As they managed their finances, Tim and Emma learned about budgeting. They realized that setting financial goals and planning their spending helped them make more thoughtful choices.

One day, Tim saw a cool new gadget in the store. He was tempted to spend all his money on it, but he remembered his goal of saving for a special outing with his friends. "I'll wait a little longer," he said, feeling proud of his self-control.

Emma faced a comparable situation when she spotted a beautiful art set. "It's so tempting," she said, "but I really want to save up for an art class I've been eyeing." With determination, she put the art set back on the shelf.

As they practiced delayed gratification, Tim and Emma discovered that by saving and budgeting, they could achieve their goals and make their dreams come true.

With their newfound financial skills and the help of Chores for Dough, Tim and Emma not only earned money but also learned the value of hard work, discipline, and giving back.

They felt like they were becoming true money masters, using their earnings wisely and being responsible with their finances. Their piggy banks were filling up, and their hearts were brimming with joy and a sense of accomplishment.

And so, with the power of Chores for Dough and the magic of financial wisdom, Tim and Emma continued their money adventure, ready to take on new challenges, earn more dough, and make every penny count.

CHAPTER 10: MONEY ADVENTURES WITH FRIENDS

Tim and Emma's money journey had become a thrilling adventure, and they couldn't wait to share their knowledge with their friends. They decided to host a "Money Adventure Day" and invite all their friends to join in the fun.

"Hey, guys! Guess what? We're going on a money adventure!" Tim exclaimed, rallying his friends at the playground. Emma chimed in, "We'll learn about saving, spending, and even investing!"

Their friends were curious and excited to take part. The day of the Money Adventure arrived, and the park was buzzing with laughter and chatter.

Nana May, always up for a grand time, joined in as their guide. She handed out colorful activity booklets filled with puzzles, quizzes, and interactive money challenges.

Their first stop was the "Budgeting Booth," where each friend was given a mock allowance and a list of things they wanted to buy. With Nana May's guidance, they learned to create budgets and decide which items to prioritize.

"It's like a real-life shopping spree!" Emma said, looking at her budget sheet. Tim added, "But we have to be smart about how we spend our money."

Next, they visited the "Savings Station," where they learned about the magic of compound interest. Nana May showed them how a little money saved over time could grow into something big.

"Wow, money can multiply itself?" one of their friends exclaimed. Nana May nodded, "Exactly! The longer you keep your money in savings, the more it can grow through interest."

The kids were in awe of the power of saving, and they all vowed to start their own piggy banks at home.

At the "Entrepreneur Corner," Tim and Emma shared their experiences with their candy stock market game. They instructed their friends about investing and the joy of watching their money grow through smart choices.
"I'm going to start my own business too!" one of their friends said, inspired by their entrepreneurial spirit.

Next came the "Giving Grove," where they learned about the joy of giving back. Nana May shared heartwarming stories of how even small acts of kindness could make a significant difference in someone's life.

"I never thought about helping others with my money before," one of their friends said. "It feels really good!"

As the Money Adventure Day ended, the kids gathered around Nana May for a special surprise. She handed each of them a small seedling.

"What's this for, Nana?" Tim asked, holding the seedling in his hand. Nana May smiled, "This seedling is a symbol of your money adventures. Just like you care for this plant and watch it grow, remember to nurture your financial knowledge and watch your money grow over time."

The kids felt a sense of wonder as they cradled their seedlings. They realized that their money adventures were just like planting seeds—every lesson, every experience, and every decision was a step towards a brighter financial future.

As they bid farewell to their friends, Tim and Emma knew that they had sparked a spark of curiosity and excitement about money in their friends' hearts.

With Nana May by their side and their friends joining in the fun, their money adventure had become a shared journey of growth, learning, and friendship.

And so, with their seedlings in hand and their spirits soaring, Tim and Emma continued their money adventure, knowing that with every step they took, they were sowing the seeds of financial wisdom and embarking on a lifetime of smart money choices.

CHAPTER 11: THE GREAT MONEY DETECTIVE ADVENTURE

One sunny afternoon, Tim and Emma stumbled upon an old, dusty treasure chest in the attic. Curiosity got the better of them, and they opened it to find a collection of mysterious old coins and bills.

"Woah! Look at all this cool money!" Tim said, marveling at the ancient coins. Emma spotted an old map buried beneath the currency. "I think this is a treasure map!" she exclaimed.

Nana May joined in the excitement, "You know what, kids? I think we have stumbled upon a thrilling money detective adventure!"

With their detective hats on, they examined the old map closely. It led to a series of locations in their town, and they were convinced that a treasure awaited them at the end of the trail.

As they followed the map's clues, they learned about the history of money, from ancient coins to modern banknotes. Each location held a puzzle or riddle that they had to solve to unlock the next clue.

At the first stop, they found themselves in front of a majestic old building. "This must be the town's first bank!" Emma said, reading the plaque.

Nana May shared stories of how banks were set up and how people used to keep their money safe. "Banks are like money guardians, keeping our hard- earned cash secure," she said.

With their first clue in hand, they ventured to the next stop—the bustling market square. "Here's where people used to trade goods before money was invented!" Tim exclaimed, pointing to a historical marker.

They met an old market vendor who challenged them to a math game. "Solve this puzzle, and you shall receive the next clue!" he said with a grin.

The kids put their money skills to the test, and soon enough, they cracked the code and moved on to the next location.

At the town museum, they uncovered more fascinating facts about the evolution of money, from bartering to the first coins minted. They marveled at ancient artifacts and learned how money had shaped societies throughout history.

As their adventure continued, they visited the town's first stock exchange and even a hidden coin minting workshop.

At each location, they collected ancient coins and bills as souvenirs. "These will be our treasure tokens!" Emma said, tucking them safely into a little pouch.

Finally, they arrived at the last clue, which led them to a majestic old tree in the heart of the town park. Under the tree, they found a chest filled with shiny coins and sparkling gems.

"We found the treasure!" Tim and Emma exclaimed; their eyes gleaming with delight.

Nana May smiled, "You see, kids, the real treasure wasn't just the shiny coins and gems. It was the knowledge and experience you gained on this money detective adventure."

They realized that through their quest, they had learned about the history of money, the importance of saving and investing, and the value of being resourceful.

As they counted their treasure tokens, they decided to donate a part to a local charity. "We're sharing our treasure, just like we learned about giving back!" Emma said proudly.

With their money detective adventure ending, Tim and Emma felt a sense of accomplishment and gratitude. They knew that the experience had not only been thrilling but had also deepened their understanding of money and its impact on the world.

As they bid farewell to the old coins and bills, they knew that their adventure was just one chapter in their ongoing money journey. With Nana May as their guide and the spirit of curiosity in their hearts, they were ready to embark on more exciting money adventures in the future.

And so, with their money detective hats held high and their eyes shining with wonder, Tim and Emma continued their money journey, knowing that the greatest treasure of all was the knowledge and wisdom they had gained along the way.

CHAPTER 12: THE MYSTERY OF THE SECRET SAVINGS CLUB

Tim and Emma's money adventures were full of surprises, but nothing could have prepared them for the mystery they stumbled upon—the Secret Savings Club!

One day, as they were playing in the backyard, they discovered a hidden door beneath a pile of leaves. "Hey, what's this?" Tim said, brushing off the leaves to reveal a small, mysterious door.

Emma's eyes widened, "I wonder where it leads." With a sense of excitement, they opened the door and found themselves in a hidden underground chamber.

It was a treasure trove of piggy banks, money jars, and stacks of coins. "This must be the Secret Savings Club!" Tim whispered.

Suddenly, they heard a voice behind them, "Welcome to the Secret Savings Club, young savers!" It was an old man with twinkling eyes and a mischievous grin.

He introduced himself as Mr. Pennywise, the keeper of the Secret Savings Club. "This place holds the knowledge of generations of savers," he said, "and you two have stumbled upon its secret."

Mr. Pennywise explained that the Secret Savings Club was a gathering place for savers of all ages. It was a place where people shared their money wisdom, learned from one another, and celebrated their financial victories.

Tim and Emma felt like they had entered a magical world of money knowledge. Mr. Pennywise showed them ancient scrolls filled with money wisdom passed down through the ages.

"You see, young savers, money is not just about numbers and coins," he said. "It's about values, discipline, and understanding the true meaning of wealth."

He taught them about the power of compound interest, the importance of setting financial goals, and the joy of watching their savings grow over time. As they explored the Secret Savings Club, they met fellow savers of all ages — children, parents, and even grandparents—all eager to share their money stories.

They heard tales of people achieving their dreams through smart saving and investing. They learned about families working together to reach financial goals and the joy of passing down money wisdom from one generation to the next.

Mr. Pennywise showed them a special section of the club called the "Kindness Corner." Here, savers would use a part of their savings to help others in need.

"Being rich isn't just about having lots of money," Mr. Pennywise said. "It's about having a generous heart and using your wealth to make a positive impact in the world."

Tim and Emma felt inspired by the stories they heard and the lessons they learned. They knew that they were part of something special—a community of savers who understood the true value of money.

As they prepared to leave the Secret Savings Club, Mr. Pennywise handed them each a small key. "This key symbolizes the knowledge and wisdom you have gained today," he said.

"Keep it safe and remember that the true treasure lies within you—the power to make smart money choices, to save for your dreams, and to use your wealth to bring joy and kindness to others."

With their hearts full of gratitude and their minds brimming with new knowledge, Tim and Emma stepped out of the Secret Savings Club.

As they closed the small, mysterious door behind them, they knew that they were part of something extraordinary. They were part of a community of savers who understood that money was not about what you had—it was about the values you held, the dreams you pursued, and the impact you made on the world.

And so, with the key to the Secret Savings Club held close to their hearts, Tim and Emma continued their money journey, knowing that they were part of a timeless legacy of savers, united by the power of wisdom and the joy of making every penny count.

CHAPTER 13: THE MAGICAL MONEY TREE

One day, as Tim and Emma were playing in the backyard, they noticed a peculiar-looking tree. Its leaves sparkled like gold, and its branches were laden with shiny coins.

"Whoa, check out this tree!" Tim exclaimed, his eyes wide with wonder. Emma touched one of the coins, and it felt cool to the touch, as if it had just been minted.

Nana May came out to join them and chuckled, "Looks like you've found the magical money tree!"

"The magical money trees?" Emma asked, her curiosity piqued. "Does that mean it gives us money?"

Nana May winked, "Well, let's find out!" She explained that the tree was said to have special powers, granting wishes related to money and financial dreams.

"But" Nana May cautioned, "the magical money tree only grants wish to those who understand the true value of money and use it responsibly."

Tim and Emma thought hard about their wishes. They knew that money was not about buying toys or treats—it was about creating opportunities, achieving dreams, and helping others too.

They each decided to make a wish. Tim closed his eyes and wished for a savings account that would grow magically with every deposit he made. "I want to save up for my college education and have enough for any unexpected emergencies too," he said.

Emma's wish was for a special art scholarship that would allow her to attend art classes and workshops. "I want to become an amazing artist and share my talent with the world," she said with determination.

With their wishes made, they waited in anticipation. Suddenly, a gust of wind rustled the leaves of the magical money tree, and they saw a shimmering light surround them.
The next morning, as they checked their piggy banks, they were amazed. Tim's savings account had grown magically overnight, and Emma received an invitation to a prestigious art scholarship program.

Their wishes had come true!

But the magic did not stop there. They noticed that the magical money tree had another surprise in store. The coins on its branches began to multiply, and they found more money lying around the yard.

"It's like a treasure hunt!" Tim laughed, collecting the coins with excitement.

Nana May smiled, "The magical money tree is rewarding you for being responsible with your wishes. It's a reminder that when you use money wisely, it can bring even more abundance into your life."

From that day on, Tim and Emma treated the magical money tree with care and gratitude. They continued to make thoughtful wishes, not just for themselves but also for their family and friends.

They used their magical money gifts to support local charities, help their community, and make small acts of kindness to brighten someone's day.

Word of the magical money tree spread, and soon, their neighbors and friends also made their way to the backyard, hoping for a touch of its enchantment.

With Nana May's guidance, they all learned the true magic of money—the power to create positive change, the joy of saving and investing for the future, and the happiness of sharing their wealth with others.

As the days turned into months, the magical money tree continued to bless them with its gifts. But the greatest gift of all was the wisdom they had gained —the knowledge that money had the power to bring dreams to life, to make a difference in the world, and to create a legacy of abundance and kindness.

And so, with the magical money tree as their guide and the spirit of gratitude in their hearts, Tim and Emma continued their money journey, knowing that true magic was not in the tree itself, but in the love, responsibility, and generosity it inspired in them.

CHAPTER 14: THE GREAT MONEY FAIR

Tim and Emma's money adventures had taken them on thrilling journeys, and now it was time to share their knowledge with the whole town. They decided to host a "Great Money Fair" where everyone could come together to learn, have fun, and celebrate the magic of money.

The fair was set up in the town square, adorned with colorful banners and decorations. Tim and Emma, wearing their money detective hats, greeted the visitors with enthusiasm.

"Step right up, folks! Welcome to the Great Money Fair!" Tim called out, waving to the crowd.

Emma chimed in, "Come learn about saving, spending, investing, and giving!"

There were different booths at the fair, each offering a unique money adventure. At the "Savings Safari," kids played games to learn about the importance of saving for future goals.

At the "Entrepreneur Extravaganza," young minds highlighted their creative ideas and inventions, selling handmade crafts and treats.

Nana May hosted the "Budgeting Bonanza," where families learned to create budgets and make smart financial choices.

Tim and Emma's friends had set up the "Kindness Corner," where people could take part in acts of kindness, from writing thank-you notes to helping local charities.

At the "Investing Oasis," visitors played the candy stock market game, learning about the power of investing and patience.

As the fair went on, they also held workshops and presentations, with experts from the community sharing their money wisdom.

The town's bank manager talked about the basics of opening a savings account, while a local entrepreneur shared stories of how she turned a small business into a success.

At the end of the fair, they had a grand ceremony—the "Money Master Awards." Tim and Emma presented awards to those who had shown exceptional money skills and kindness throughout the fair.

"I am proud to present the 'Money Master Award' to our friend Jack, who started his own gardening business to save up for a new bike!" Emma announced, with a beaming smile.

Tim added, "And the 'Kindness Champion Award' goes to Sarah, who used her savings to help local families in need."

As the winners received their awards, the crowd cheered and applauded, celebrating the achievements of their fellow townspeople.

The fair had brought the town together, fostering a sense of community and camaraderie. Families exchanged money tips, kids excitedly shared their financial goals, and the town's spirit of generosity soared.

As the sun began to set, Tim and Emma felt a sense of fulfillment. They had created something magical—the Great Money Fair had not only been a fun- filled event but also a celebration of learning, sharing, and growing together.

With hearts full of gratitude, they thanked Nana May and their friends for their support. "You've all been a part of our amazing money journey," Tim said, "and we couldn't have done it without you!"

Emma added, "Remember, money isn't just about numbers—it's about dreams, goals, and the joy of making a difference in each other's lives."

And so, with the memories of the Great Money Fair etched in their hearts, Tim and Emma continued their money adventure, knowing that they had touched the lives of their town and had sown the seeds of financial wisdom, one magical moment at a time.

The End...

EPILOGUE: THE NEVER-ENDING MONEY ADVENTURE

As the days turned into weeks and the weeks into months, Tim and Emma's money adventure continued with boundless enthusiasm and curiosity. They had learned so much, but they knew that there was always more to discover.

Their backyard had become a treasure trove of money knowledge, filled with memories of the magical money tree, the Secret Savings Club, and the Great Money Fair. It was a constant reminder of the joy of learning and growing together.

Nana May remained their wise guide, sharing stories and wisdom that had no end. She encouraged them to dream big, to believe in their potential, and to use their money skills to make the world a better place.

With each new lesson, they felt their confidence grow. Tim began reading books about finance and investing, dreaming of a future where he could start his own business. Emma's art flourished as she attended the art classes she had wished for, and she even sold some of her artwork to fund a community art project.

Together, they continued to save, invest, and share their wealth with others, making a positive impact in their community and beyond.

Their friends had joined in the money adventure too, forming a close-knit group that shared their financial dreams and supported each other every step of the way.

Their piggy banks, once filled with a few coins, were now overflowing with a sense of accomplishment and joy. They knew that every penny counted, not just for themselves but for the dreams they held dear and the causes they cared about.

As they gazed at the stars one night, Tim and Emma marveled at how far their money journey had taken them. They had grown into money masters, with hearts full of kindness, minds brimming with knowledge, and a spirit of gratitude that knew no bounds.

"We'll never stop learning and exploring," Tim said, his eyes shining with determination.

Emma nodded, "Our money adventure will go on forever, and we'll keep inspiring others to join in too!"

Nana May smiled, knowing that their money adventure had only just begun. "Remember, my dear adventurers, the magic of money lies not in the coins or bills, but in the power, it holds to shape your dreams and the lives of others," she said.

With hearts filled with love, friendship, and the joy of discovery, Tim and Emma knew that their money adventure was indeed never-ending.

And so, under the vast night sky, they made a promise to each other and to themselves—to keep exploring, keep learning, and keep spreading the magic of money to everyone they met.

And as they set off on another chapter of their money adventure, they knew that with the spirit of curiosity, the guidance of wisdom, and the power of friendship, they could achieve anything they set their minds to.

And so, with hearts full of love and excitement, Tim and Emma's money adventure continued, one step, one coin, and one magical moment at a time.

BOOKS BY THIS AUTHOR

Echoes Of Despair Battling The Celestial Menace

In the vast expanse of the cosmos, amidst the countless galaxies that dance across the velvet tapestry of space, a shadowy menace lurks. A threat so profound and insurmountable that it has the potential to reduce our beloved planet to nothing but a desolate wasteland. Unbeknownst to humanity, a meteor of cataclysmic proportions hurtles through the abyss, aiming to extinguish life as we know it. But amidst the shadows of despair, a glimmer of hope emerges, calling upon the resilience of the human spirit and our ability to face the unimaginable.

"Echoes of Despair: Battling the Celestial Menace" unveils an extraordinary tale that transcends the boundaries of our world. It begins with an unexpected visitation, as enigmatic beings from a distant galaxy descend upon Earth, their presence cloaked in mystery and trepidation. With grave urgency, they convey a dire warning—a gargantuan meteor, colossal in size, approaches with a trajectory set for our fragile blue planet.

The Awakening Wave: Embracing Collective Consciousness

The Awakening Wave invites readers to envision a world where individualism is no longer the driving force, but rather a collective consciousness becomes the driving factor for human progress. This book explores the power of interconnectedness, the beauty of shared experiences, and the potential for a harmonious coexistence between humanity and this enigmatic species from the ocean depths.

www.ingramcontent.com/pod-product-compliance
Lightning Source LLC
Chambersburg PA
CBHW060849260726
48661CB00002B/701